T0277145

Plague
Poems

Plague Poems is published by Little Wing.

ISBN 978-1-877484-98-8

202110251404

Plague
Poems

Brian Flaherty

It is as reasonable to represent one kind of imprisonment by another, as it is to represent anything that really exists by that which exists not.

Daniel Defoe

1

The change of season can only be detected in the sky
The speed with which night falls and the quality
Of pleasure demand good health
Men and woman consume each other rapidly
In the evening we walk along the same boulevard
Or else come out on to our balconies
At first sight a town without inkling
How we work here, how we love and how we die
With back turned to the bay
It is impossible to see the sea
You are gathering strength for the journey
You smile
I'm feeling fine you say
I kiss your slightly moist forehead
The smile follows me towards the door.

2

You see, I am keeping a lookout
Talking the language of Saint Just
Rubbing my neck in a mechanical way
I find you out of bed wearing a suit
And with makeup disguising your pallor
Yes, you say, your eyes shining
We'll start again
In any event, our townspeople
Have started to become concerned
The evening papers picking up the matter.

3

More than one person
Walking at night along the pavement
People call for radical measures
Accusing the authorities of inaction
Old Michel's eyes are shining, and he
Whistles as he breathes
Like a healthy man whose thick blood
Has suddenly rebelled against him
Something threatening in this phenomenon
The extent and origin not yet clear
It must be an epidemic the priest says
His eyes smiling behind his glasses
The following day an already warm breeze
Is blowing, a scent of flowers
From the most distant suburbs
On the left-hand door I read the words
Come in, I'm hanged in red chalk.

4

He played music for the choir
It wears you out, always blowing down a tube
As if something rising from the depths
Of the earth were constantly calling
Going out of your way
To view people and things through the
Large end of the telescope, to become
The historian of that which has no history
Some dryness of heart
A mass of minor details
Which are none the less important
But the fact remains, you say
When you're ill
You shouldn't blow down a tube.

5

White butterflies
The man then tears up little pieces of paper
Above the street, and the creatures
Attracted by this shower of white butterflies
Come out into the middle of the road
Raising enquiring paws towards the last pieces of paper
At this, he spits on the cats
Firmly and accurately
And as one of his gobs of saliva hits the target
He laughs.

6

Question:

How can one manage not to lose time?

Answer:

Experience it at its full length

Means:

Spend days in the dentist's waiting-room

On an uncomfortable chair

Listen to lectures in a language that one

Doesn't understand

Choose the most round about and least

Convenient routes

Live on one's balcony on a Sunday afternoon.

7

Today the little old man opposite
Is very put out
There are no more cats.

8

Neither more or less than a fever
The whole town has a high temperature
You decide you must quickly try to sort out your head
A white wooden shelf
With two or three dictionaries on it
A blackboard on which one can still read
The half-effaced inscription
*Paths of flower*s
You are fussy about the form of words
Finally agree on *personal sorrows*
Though the sky is blue it has a dull sheen
Softening as the afternoon goes.

9

A long succession of the extraordinary
The old images of pestilence:
Athens stricken, abandoned by its birds
The convicts of Marseille
Piling dripping corpses into a hole
Beds, damp and rotten, sticking to the earth floor
Of the hospital in Constantinople
The living copulating in the cemeteries of Milan
Chinese towns full of people dying in silence
The rest hanging by threads
And imperceptible movements.

10

Fingering the page of statistics in your pocket
You are still trying to find the right words
It's not a matter of painting a black picture
It's a matter of taking precautions
Even to express such simple emotions
Costs an enormous effort
Most of all you like a certain bell in the neighbourhood
That rings softly around five in the evening.

11

A man who has something on his conscience
Little white posters
Stuck up in the least obstructive corners
We are advised to
Observe the most rigorous hygiene
Agree to isolation
Undergo a health test
Declare any cases
Your favourite remark, *big fish always eat little one*s
One day when the grocer appears less friendly
I return home in a quite disproportionate fit of anger.

12

It remains compulsory to declare the disease
And isolate patients
Growing inside me the slight sense of dizziness
They are talking about us in offices
Writing our names on index cards
As every evening, a light breeze
Brings the hum of voices
The great roars of invisible boats and the murmur
That arises from the sea
My voice is hoarse and I have difficulty forming words
You find it hard to rise out of your seat
Stay there, looking at the dark street
Stars appearing and disappearing in the black sky.

13

From this point on it has become the affair of us all
Creatures bound together by mutual sympathy
By flesh and heart
We are reduced to wandering our mournful town
Day after day, engaged in illusory games of memory
This hollow, this precise emotion
By means of these dead words
In short, from now on accepting
Our status as prisoners.

14

To make the trains run again in our imagination
The only way to escape this unbearable holiday
To speak more particularly at last of lovers
Those one sees wandering at any time of the day
Subservient to the sun and the rain
Handed over to the whims of the heavens
To go back through the story
And examine its imperfections
It must be said that people are drinking a lot
You have the impression that cars
Have started to go round in circles.

15

The rest of the story he said, *is very simple*
This is how it is for everyone
You get married
You stay in love for a while
And you work
You work so much that you forget to love.

16

Evening is coming
We walk together along the steeply descending streets
Between the blue, ochre and violet walls of the houses
The town which had once been so busy
At this time of day, seems oddly deserted
Only a few bugle calls in the still golden sky
Show that the army is pretending to do its job.

17

At a certain moment I ought to have
Found the words
That would have kept her
But I couldn't.

18

The ecclesiastical authorities have decided to wage war
By their own means, a week of collective prayer
I am aware only of the hard indifference
That starts to fill me
This feeling of a heart slowly closing around itself
In spite of everything you have told me…
In any event it can't do any harm.

19

After a short pause, his voice lowers
My brethren
In the vast granary of the universe
The implacable flail
Will thresh the human corn until
The chaff is divided from the grain.

20

A sky, in which water mingles with sunshine
Casting a fresh light across the square
In front of us a stranger
Laughing noiselessly with his eyes shut
Soon there will only be mad people in our town
Let's have a drink.

21

Down on the terrace
In front of a glass of warm beer
I read the newspaper decrees
The disobedient threatened with prison
Watching the faces of the passers-by
Their expressions of melancholy
The pictures are the hardest to bear
A landscape of old stone and water.

22

Every day that goes by brings each of us
Provided we don't die
Closer to the end of our troubles
The nearby sea is out of bounds
The body no longer has the right to enjoy it
Instead we walk aimlessly through the yellow streets
And in this way we reach evening.

23

Dusk spreads through the room like grey water
The pink of the evening sky
Reflected against windows and mirrors
In the middle of the empty room
You seem like a lost shade.

24

To be able to plunge into a dreamless sleep
Like the woman who
In an empty district
Suddenly throws open a window above her
And lets out two great cries
Before pulling the shutters closed again
On the deep shadows of her room.

I am in darkness trying to see the light
On the boulevard, a cranky old man wearing a felt hat
And a large tie, repeating endlessly
God is great, come to Him
And do you *believe?* you ask me
Looking out the window into the deserted street
I don't know what awaits me
Or what will come after all this
At the beginning
When it was a sickness like any other
Religion had its place
But now we see that it is serious
We remember pleasure
In the blazing dusk
All the anguish imprinted on our faces
Resolving into a crazed excitement.

26

The town is silent, inhabited only by rustling noises
In the distance, where the horizon condenses
Into a darker mass, we sense the presence of the sea
I feel my exhaustion and at the same time
Struggle against a sudden, unreasonable
Desire to confide
I don't know anything more than that
Our victories will always be temporary
Perhaps it is better for God
That we should not believe in him
Without raising our eyes to heaven and to His silence
Far, far away, the siren of an ambulance sounds.

I can't concentrate
Don't know how to resolve the end of my sentence
Every evening I sort out the card index
Translate it into diagrams
To present the situation in as precise a way
As is possible
Sometimes at midnight
In the great stillness of the deserted town
Just as we get into bed, you switch on the radio
Seeking news from distant parts of the world
A smile slowly crossing your face.

28

On the left there is a green-painted shop
Shaded by a slanting awning
Made of coarse yellow cloth
In front of the large door people are stationed
A radio which has been softly droning out
Sentimental songs
Announces the victims from the previous day
You look at the sky for a second
We go on in silence.

29

The war memorial is situated on a promenade
Which for quite a short distance
Runs along the cliffs overlooking the port
You attentively read the list of those
Who have died on the field of honour
We are starting to get old
We have to take advantage of everything
I lean over the parapet, absorbed
In contemplating the bare, deserted quays
A vague scent of humidity still rising from the lawns.

The woman explains:
Too many people are not doing anything
The epidemic is everyone's business
We all have to do our duty
I put on the lights, sit down at the table
A breeze gently lifting the curtains
Over the french windows
The sound of Saint James's Infirmary Blues
Pouring out from a gramophone
Perched up near the ceiling
I notice my hand is trembling and decide
That undoubtedly, I am altogether drunk
This dreadful burning
Eating away at my temples.

31

You still haven't understood she says
Shrugging her shoulders
The gilded sun rising behind
The houses in the east.

32

The inhabitant accuses the wind
That wraps her legs in seaweed and salt
It is shuffling the cards
Week in, week out, prisoners
Struggling along as best we can
The disease that brings us together
In the solidarity of lovers under siege
At the same time drives us back into solitude
Hastening down the street, bent forward
The empty town groaning like
An island of the damned.

33

After eleven, plunged into darkness
Under a moonlit sky
The town is like a monument
A necropolis in which disease and stone
Have finally silenced every voice
Night crouching in our hearts
The myths that are passed around
Black shape of a tree, the howl of a dog.

34

The days are an endless trampling
Thousands of shoes marching to the rhythm
A monotony that flattens everything in its path
Your face has lost its flesh
The details of colour that memory keeps
A spiritual and physical emaciation
In truth, everything becomes the present
The whole town is a waiting room
Inhabited by people asleep on our feet.

It is a case of marking time, kicking our heels
Mist, heat and rain follow one another in the sky
Silent flocks of starlings and thrushes
Coming from the south
Fly overhead but skirt around the town
As though keeping their distance
We have discovered how tired we are
Liable to sudden moments of emotion
Or falling silent, giving evasive answers to questions
My only defense, to harden myself
Tighten the knot which has formed
Avoiding any gesture that is not absolutely necessary
There is no room for sentimentality
When you have only slept for four hours
A thread of saliva running between half-open lips.

36

Again we plunge into the uncontrolled tide
Heads lowered, elbow to elbow
Imprisoned between the sky and the walls of this town
Immersing ourselves in its contradictions
We are complicit in everything we see
The black and the white, silhouettes against the light
You have made an accomplice of me
Hungry for human warmth that draws us together
This manner of silence like leaving a church
Or funeral chamber
Have you noticed you ask me
That you cannot accumulate illnesses?
You know very well you cannot trust me.

37

I go to bed late and sleep a heavy sleep
In the dream I am running
To the highest part of the town, and there
From a little square, call to her
With a great cry across the town walls
She takes out two gauze masks
Offers me one and puts on the other
When I speak the mask puffs out
And grows damp around my mouth
The conversation slightly unreal, like a dialogue
Between statues
We can't heal and know at the same time
So let's heal as fast as we can
That's the most urgent thing
At the door she turns suddenly around
I see for the first time since the outbreak
She is crying.

38

The woman begins to say something
But has to cough in order to finish it
Her voice suddenly starting to crack
She slumps back on the bench between dusty trees
Watching the branches and the blue morning sky
Gradually getting back her breath
Forgive me. But tiredness is a form of madness
You see, she says, deliberately not meeting my eye
Even God himself cannot separate us now.

39

We have replaced our ordinary observances
With irrational superstitions and predictions
Based on bizarre calculations
The number of the year, the number of deaths
The number of months already passed
Some consult Nostradamus and Saint Odile daily
Announcing a series of apocalyptic events
Prophecies by wise men and saints
Appear in the newspapers
Read with as much eagerness as love stories.

40

A sharp wind pours through the half-open door
Striking me full in the face
It brings inside the smell of rain
Of damp pavements which warn us
Even before we go out
Walking in front, you have difficulty
In keeping hold of your headgear
Large clouds speeding from one end
Of the horizon to the other
Cast shadows over the houses before
The cold, golden light returns.

41

We cannot predict anything for certain
In a town shut in on itself, nothing remains secret
Incidents and conflicts grow more frequent
Lighting and fanning flames in our chests
Nothing left for it but to be quiet and watchful
A few metres apart, arms hanging by our sides
As foreign to one another as if quarantined
On different planets, sniffing the luminous air
The faint scent of spice and stone.

42

In a sky, swept clean and shining by the wind
The distant lighthouse adds its brief ember
Three times reappearing in the darkness
I have always wanted to escape
Chewing the nails of just one hand, the right
Silence falling back on us
With all its weight of sky and stars.

43

Shortly before we arrive the smell of iodine
And seaweed tells us we are here
The muffled breathing of the waves against the cliff
A soft hissing at the foot of the great blocks of the jetty
We sit down on the rocks facing out to sea
Feel the pitted face of rock under our fingers
I am filled with a strange happiness.

44

The general statistics show a decline in the disease
The longer we wait, the longer we are able to wait
Glued to a shop window of sculpted wooden toys
Tears running in a steady stream down your face
There is a language you have forgotten
You raise a limp hand, say very deliberately
In a strange, hollow voice
No one in the world, no one, is immune.

45

We react in contradictory ways
Moving from excitement to depression
The streets still silent by day
Are invaded in the evenings
Overcoats and scarves spilling out into the streets
The infection is retreating all along the line
Abandoning its position
A rent appearing in this opaque veil
That for months has surrounded us
The cold has set in and yet the sky
Has never been so blue.

46

My reticence, your habit of expressing
Everything in simple sentences
In the evening we make a furtive sortie
To buy what we need
Emerging from the shops to hurry down streets
Where cats are warming themselves
In last patches of autumn sun
One cannot forget everything
With the best will in the world.

47

The woman is knitting, meticulously
She examines a dubious stitch at the end of her needle
Raising her head to look out the window
In the street, hurried footsteps
Fleeing in front of a distant rumbling
A storm approaches
Threshing the sky above us with its flail
Great awnings flapping an invisible war.

48

Always the same pause, the same solemn interval
The same lull that follows a battle
I lean towards you, put my hand for a moment
On your damp, twisted hair
Time slowing down, held in suspension
A magnificent new day rising over the port.

49

The time of forgetting has not yet begun
For those who have looked beyond humanity
To something that they could not even imagine
There has been no reply.

Desire comes unbridled
The chronicle is drawing to a close
The front of the house gilded by the last
Rays of the sun
A dirty spaniel trots along by the wall
Reaches our door, pauses
Sits down on its hindquarters
And turns around to start eating its own fleas
The only sounds we can hear are intermittent
Bursts of music from the centre of the town
The only certainties we have in common
Love, suffering and exile
But what does it mean, the plague?
It's life, that's all
When I reach for you,
Night has already swallowed
The whole sky.

Just before midnight on 25 March 2020 the country entered its first Covid lockdown, and for seven weeks in the great stillness of the deserted town the pandemic was everyone's business. On the first morning I pulled Albert Camus' *The Plague* (*La Peste*) from the bookshelf and started a daily routine: to read five pages, sample and shape into a poem that echoed our situation, and email to a friend. These are those 50 poems.

Thanks
    To Murrow my publisher, my oldest friend.
    To Michele for her kind support.
    And most of all to *ma famille en confinement*,
    Annie & Paddy.

Milton Keynes UK
Ingram Content Group UK Ltd.
UKHW041258121124
2786UKWH00023B/91